Eyam & District

Guide &

Rob

AE

Nether
Padley

Grindleford

Eyam

Foolow

Froggatt

A625

A623

Calver   Curbar

Baslow

Hassop

A619

A619

Foolow

1

6

P WC   P PAY & DISPLAY   P FREE

Grindleford

2

4

3

† Church

N

W — E

S

The
Square

5

Stoney
Middleton

Boundary
Stone

Grindleford

Eyam

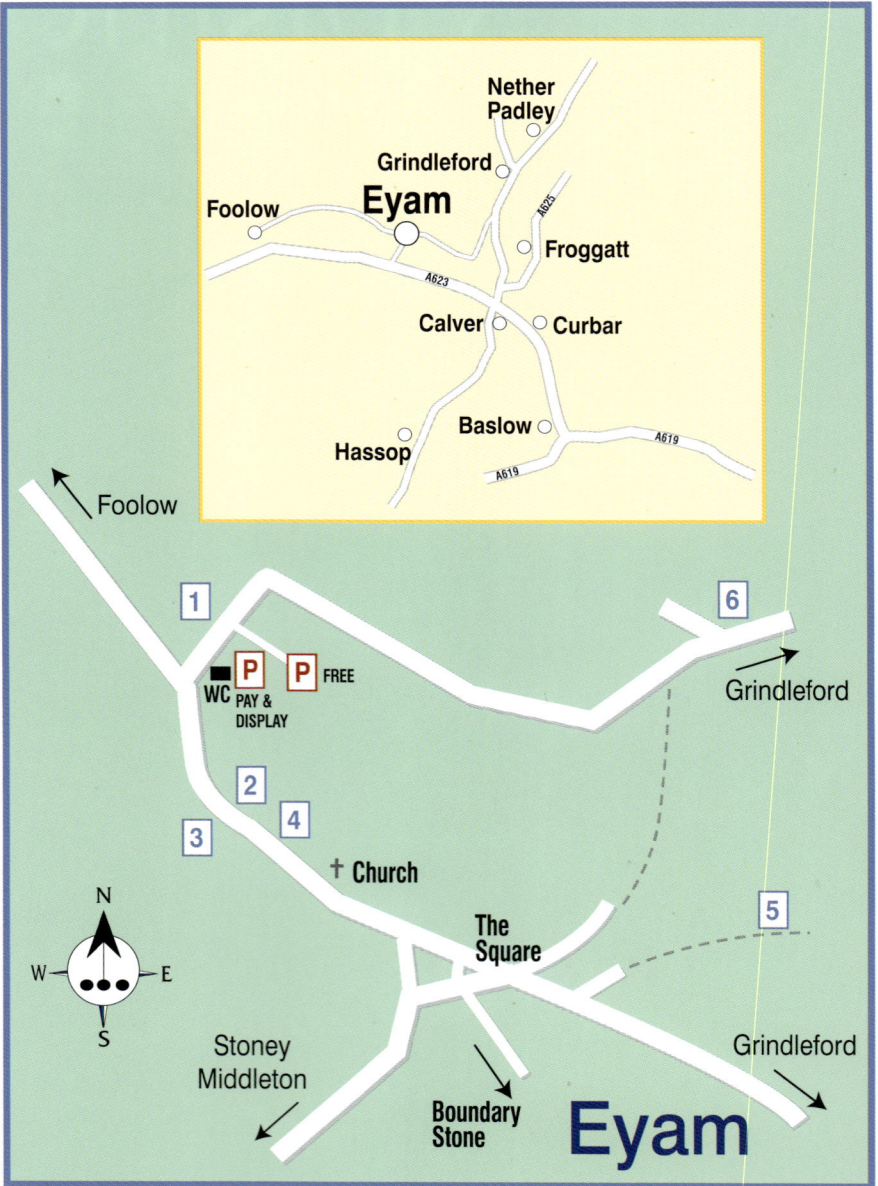

1	Eyam Museum	4	Plague Cottages
2	Eyam Hall	5	Riley Graves
3	Village Stocks	6	Mompesson's Well

EYAM AND DISTRICT

INCLUDING CALVER, BASLOW, FOOLOW, GRINDLEFORD, STONEY MIDDLETON, FROGGATT AND HASSOP

Eyam: The Plague Village

Eyam (pronounced "Eem" as in "stream") cannot escape from its slightly morbid past, as it seems it will always be saddled with the epithet of "The Plague Village." The heroic self-imposed quarantine by the villagers after the Plague struck during the years 1665–66 has been called "the greatest epic in the annals of rural life," and the village is always associated with the tragic 'visitation.' (see box)

But despite its tragic past, Eyam is a lively, bustling village today, and the Victorian **Village Institute** opposite the church is still the centre for most social activities, including a sell-out annual village pantomime at Christmas time.

The restored 13th century **Parish Church of St Lawrence** has many touching memorials of the Plague years, including a book recording the names of all

Above left: Parish Church of St Lawrence, Eyam **Right top**: Sundial, Eyam church **Bottom:** The Plague Window, Eyam Church

3

The head of the cross in Eyam churchyard

Plague Cottages, Eyam

the victims and the chair of William Mompesson, the rector who led the villagers in their selfless act of heroism three centuries ago. This was rescued from a Liverpool antique shop. Among the other features in this fascinating church are some medieval wall paintings, an Elizabethan altar screen and other good Jacobean woodwork, and an elaborate 18th century (1775) sundial over the south door.

Close to the magnificent, though truncated, **Saxon Preaching Cross** in the churchyard is the table-top tomb of Mompesson's wife, Catherine, who died at the height of the outbreak. Also in the churchyard is the amusing headstone to the Derbyshire and England cricketer Harry Bagshaw. It shows a set of stumps being broken by a ball, over which the celestial umpire's hand points the index finger upwards – showing that Harry's innings is well and truly over!

Opposite the tiny **Village Green**, complete with its restored **Stocks** for wrongdoers, is the late 17th century **Eyam Hall**, a lovely gritstone gabled and mullioned building which has been the home of the Wright family ever since it was built in 1676. The hall is a wonderfully intimate and lived-in house, and guided tours are available throughout the summer months. Don't miss the exceptionally fine tapestries in the upstairs rooms and the restored knot and herb garden. There is also a craft centre with shops and a buttery-type restaurant in the stables at the rear of the building.

Eyam Museum, in the former Methodist Chapel in Hawkhill Road, has award-winning exhibits and displays which graphically tell the story of the village from prehistoric to modern times, plus the harrowing story of the Eyam Plague.

The museum was inspired by Clarence Daniel, a lifelong resident and local historian who ran a small private museum in his house, but was thwarted in his attempts to set up a public museum. His collection was passed to the Village Society on his death in 1987, and Eyam Museum Ltd. was formed. Seven years later, the former Methodist Chapel became

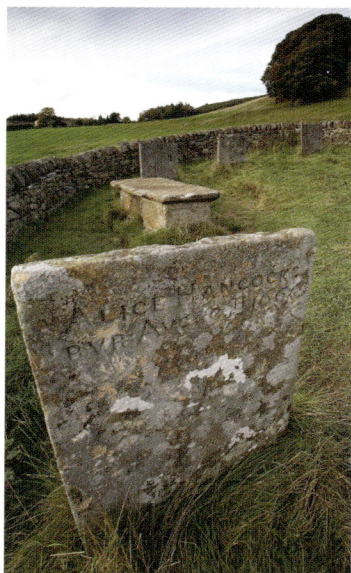
Riley Graves

available, and the museum eventually opened in 1994. The rat on the weather vane on the roof of the building gives away the guilty carrier of the Plague virus, which was transmitted to man by the fleas of the black rat.

One Eyam family which was particularly hard hit by the Plague were the Hancocks of Riley House Farm, seven of whom died within a week of each other in August, 1665. The distraught mother of the family had to bury her husband,

Eyam Hall

The Eyam Plague

In a 14-month period between September, 1665 and November, 1666, a total of 259 Eyam villagers died of the Bubonic Plague, and in some cases, whole families were wiped out. It is thought that the Plague virus arrived in Eyam in a box of cloth brought from London by George Vicars, a journeyman tailor.

Many cottages in the village are marked with plaques recording the names of the victims, ensuring that the epic story of the self-imposed sacrifice which the villagers made will never be forgotten.

Led by their minister, the Rev. William Mompesson, and his non-conformist predecessor, the Rev. Thomas Stanley, the villagers imposed a quarantine and ban on movement so that the deadly virus would not spread through the rest of the county. Some of the pitiful graves of the victims can be seen in the fields around the village, because they were not allowed to be buried in the churchyard during the "visitation."

Neighbouring parishes and the ruling landlord, the Earl of Devonshire, left supplies for villagers at special points on the village boundary, some of which can still be seen, such as Mompesson's Well, to the north of the village. Church services were also held in the open air to minimise the risk of infection, at the little limestone crag of Cucklett Delf in the dale below the village. This is where the annual Plague Commemoration Service is held on the last Sunday in August, to coincide with the village well dressings.

Modern critics have questioned whether the fatal outbreak was in fact the plague, as an epidemic of any disease was dubbed the plague in those days. They have also challenged the wisdom of the self-imposed quarantine, which resulted in a far greater death rate by concentrating the disease. Whatever the facts, medical knowledge was scant in 17th century Derbyshire, and the villagers undoubtedly took their brave action from the highest possible motives.

Above: Anniversary Service in Cucklett Delf, Eyam, August 1913 (courtesy: Eyam Museum)

three sons and three daughters in the fields close to the farm. The evocative headstones marking their graves can be seen grouped inside a walled enclosure known as the **Riley Graves** (National Trust), just a short way outside the village, off the minor road leading east towards Grindleford.

There is much more to Eyam's history than the well-known story of the Plague. Deep in the heather of Eyam Moor, reached from the minor Sir William Hill road, is the Bronze Age **Wet Withins Stone Circle** (now protected by English Heritage). There are numerous other burial mounds and clearance cairns nearby, showing that 4,000 years ago, this area was populated and important enough to attract these lasting monuments to the dead. Incidentally, when the heather is in bloom in the late summer, Eyam Moor has one of the finest displays in the Peak.

Bronze Age Barrow on Eyam Moor in late summer

Eyam Well dressings

Eyam dresses three of its wells or springs on the last Saturday in August, which coincides with the Plague Commemoration Service in Cucklett Delf and the village carnival. The late date of the well dressings means that the choice of flowers available for the Eyam dressers is often limited, however, the designs are always interesting and attract large numbers of visitors.

The largest well dressing in Eyam is the Town Head Well, which has one of the biggest screens (nine feet wide by nearly six feet tall) in the Peak District. The theme of the Eyam well dressings often commemorates the dreadful but never-to-be forgotten visitation of the Plague three centuries ago.

Calver

Sheltering in the Derwent Valley below Curbar Edge, Calver (pronounced "Carver") is a pleasant little stone-built village with some lovely old gritstone cottages and a fine 18ᵗʰ century bridge over the river.

Its most impressive building is undoubtedly **Calver Mill**, a magnificent, six-storeyed cotton mill first built in 1785. The present building mainly dates from a rebuilding following a fire of 1805. Internally it has cast-iron pillars holding up the floors which were originally of wood and there is a preserved Wheel House from the original mill.

Cotton was produced here until 1923, when it was bought by a Sheffield company which specialised in stainless steel products. Calver Mill, which is now converted to private residential accommodation, reached a far wider audience when it represented Colditz Castle in the popular BBC television series in the 1970s about the famous prisoner of war camp of the same name.

Calver Weir, a 19ᵗʰ century Grade II listed structure on the River Derwent, played a pivitol role by holding back water to power the cotton mill at Calver. At the time of writing

Left: Calver Bridge in spring

engineering work is underway to restore the weir after the Calver Weir Restoration Project was awarded £1.24m by the Heritage Lottery Fund. This means the structure will be saved, along with its associated unique cultural heritage features and important ecological habitats.

Calver Sough crossroads and the former Calver Sough Mine are at the northern end of the village, and recall the days when lead mining was an important part of the local economy. (A "sough" – pronounced "suff" – in Derbyshire is an underground drain constructed to take water away from lead mines). Nearby is the **Derbyshire Craft Centre**, which has a shop, gallery and restaurant for tourists.

Baslow

Baslow clusters beneath its own Peakland "edge" which provides fine views across the Derwent Valley towards Chatsworth House. The village has for centuries been closely associated with the Cavendish family. At **Goose Green** and **Nether End** you are close to Chatsworth and its parkland, with lodges designed by Jeffrey Wyatville. **The Devonshire Arms**, in Baslow is one of the best hotels in the Peak

The **Wellington Monument** was erected by a local Dr. Wrench to celebrate the Duke's victory at Waterloo, and the climb to the top of the isolated tor known as the **Eagle Stone** was said to be the test for every young Baslow man before he married.

Today, Baslow is a commuter village for nearby Sheffield and Chesterfield,

Parish Church of St Anne, Baslow

but it retains its village community spirit, despite the roaring traffic of the A623. The **Parish Church of St Anne** is beautifully situated by the river, and its squat broach spire dominates the village. An unusual feature is the clock face, which has the legend VICTORIA 1897 instead of numbers to mark the Queen's jubilee. Inside the church another unusual feature is preserved, the whip used to drive stray dogs out of the church during services.

Baslow has two fine bridges over the River Derwent. Nether End bridge is a neighbour of one of the few thatched cottages in the Peak District and the Bridge End bridge, near the church, dates from the 17th century and features a tiny Toll House with an entrance only three and a half feet (1m) high.

Foolow cross

Foolow

The name Foolow has nothing to do with the intelligence of its inhabitants – it comes from the Old English and probably means "multi-coloured hill". However, it remains the source of amusement that the small dry valley just to the west of Foolow is known as Silly Dale.

This small, nucleated village on the limestone plateau between Eyam and Tideswell clusters around its village pond or "mere" which in turn is watched over by a crocketed medieval cross. Foolow is a candidate for one of the prettiest villages in Derbyshire, for the large green is surrounded by some fine 17th and 18th century cottages, the most important of which are the bay-windowed, 17th century **Manor House** and the **Old Hall** (both private).

During this time of the village's heyday, lead mining combined with farming as the major occupation of the inhabitants, and there is still much evidence of their spoil heaps and shafts in the surrounding meadows.

The small **Parish Church** has an unusual dedication to St Hugh, and was built in 1888. The **Wesleyan Reform Chapel** was built in 1836 and has a grand, Tuscan-style porch and thin, lancet-type side-windows.

The village well-dressings take place in late August.

Grindleford

The name of this charming little Derwent-side village is most likely connected to the grindstones. These were made in local quarries for many years from the abrasive gritstone of the nearby "edges" of Froggatt and Curbar. As the name suggests, it probably means the ford near to where the grindstones were made.

Grindleford occupies a lovely position, between Eyam Moor and Froggatt Edge, and includes in its parish the beautiful **Padley Gorge** (National Trust), famous for its sessile oakwoods and summer migrant pied flycatchers. Also in the

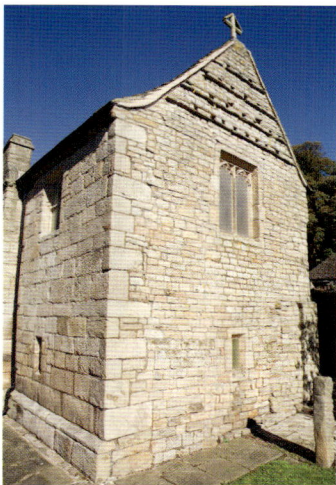

Padley Chapel

hamlet of **Upper Padley** is the simple little, barn-like structure of **Padley Chapel**, which was formerly the gatehouse of Padley Hall, the medieval manor house of the Eyre and Fitzherbert families.

It was the scene in 1588 of one of the worst of the Roman Catholic persecutions during Elizabeth I's reign. Two Catholic priests, Nicholas Garlick and Robert Ludlam, were being hidden here by Sir Thomas Fitzherbert of Norbury, however, they were discovered, arrested and taken to Derby to be hanged, drawn and quartered for their beliefs. An annual "Padley Pilgrimage" is held every July to mark this horrific deed, and the event is centred on the chapel, which was bought by the Roman Catholic Diocese of Nottingham in 1933. It

Sessile oaks, Padley Gorge

remains an evocative spot.

Nearby is the mouth of the **Totley Railway Tunnel**. Over three miles in length, it was one of the longest in Britain when it was opened in 1893, and passes under the eastern moors to Sheffield.

Grindleford village stretches for about two miles along the river and down to the fine three-arched bridge which spans the mighty Derwent. The village has a lively social life, which is reflected in the construction of the **Bishop Pavilion** near the cricket field and bridge. It was named after its major benefactor, local businessman Eric Bishop, and remains in almost constant use.

Froggatt

Froggatt stands beneath the frowning gritstone escarpment of Froggatt Edge on the well-wooded banks of the Derwent. Froggatt Show, held on August Bank Holiday Saturday, is the highlight of the year in this small village. The show has agricultural roots and was founded in the 1930s as an offshoot of the village "Cow Club". Its exhibits are now mainly horticultural, reflecting the change in village society.

Froggatt Bridge over the River Derwent dates from the 17th century and is unusual in that it has a large central arch nearer to the village and a smaller one on the other side. This most likely formed part of the original bridge constructed when the river was narrower, before the Derwent was dammed downstream for the mill at Calver.

The **Wesleyan Reform Chapel** is the major building of note in the village, which uses **All Saints Parish Church** at nearby Curbar for its Established church services.

Curbar

Although it is not as well known, Curbar had an equally tragic 'visitation' of the Plague some 33 years before it reached the more famous "Plague Village" of Eyam, across the River Derwent.

Evidence of this is provided by the collection of simple stone slabs beneath **Curbar Edge**, the gritstone escarpment which dominates the eastern side of the village. Dated 1632, they mark the graves of the Cundy family and a man called Sheldon, and there are other reminders of Plague victims just below the

View of a mist-covered Derwent Valley from Curbar Edge

Wesleyan Reform Chapel, which was built in 1862 from stone quarried from a nearby field.

Curbar today is very much a commuter village for Sheffield and Chesterfield, and its small **Parish Church of All Saints** was built in 1868. There is a circular, conical-roofed village **Lock-up** at the top end of the village, south of the main village street. This was where offenders were incarcerated by the village constable. **Stoke Hall,** about two miles to the north-west of the village, is a stately two and a half storeyed stone-built mansion with a fine Tuscan columned doorway, built in 1757. **Cliffe College** on the outskirts of the village is a modern Methodist training and conference centre, where at the end of the last century, missionaries were trained.

Hassop

Standing like a Grecian temple stranded in the heart of the Peak District, the **Roman Catholic Church of All Saints** at Hassop always comes as something of a surprise. The reason for the presence of this Classical Revival building with its Etruscan temple front and Tuscan pilasters at the rear lies just across the road at **Hassop Hall.** This elegant early 17th century house was the family seat of the staunchly-Catholic Eyre family. The church was built in 1816 and contains under its coved and coffered ceiling a wonderful painting of the Crucifixion by Lodovico Carracci, and a fine monument to its founder, Thomas

Top: The Eyre Arms, Hassop
Left: Roman Catholic Church of All Saints, Hassop

Eyre, who died in 1833.

Hassop Hall, now a hotel and restaurant, is a fine Georgian three-storeyed country house standing within its own landscaped park. Inside there are marble chimney pieces by White Watson of nearby Ashford-in-the-Water and some excellent early 19th century plasterwork. Just below the hall on the road to Bakewell stands **The Dower House**, an imposing late 17th century three-gabled house which used to be the village post office, now converted into luxury flats. **The Eyre Arms** is a popular hostelry on the road to Calver, which is clad with a vivid scarlet Virginia creeper in late summer and autumn.

Stoney Middleton

Stoney by name and stony by nature. Stoney Middleton is squeezed into the narrow valley of Middleton Dale and hemmed in by impending cliffs of limestone and the dusty quarry faces at the western end of the village.

It has a long history, which goes back to Roman times. Stoney Middleton was on the main highway between the forts at Navio (Brough) and Chesterfield, and although there is no proof of Roman usage, the restored **Roman Baths**, in **The Nook** still have the warm springs which may well have attracted passing legionnaires. Later the village became a centre for lead mining and lime burning. Old engravings now show the dale clear of trees with smoke billowing up from the lime kilns.

The **Parish Church of St Martin**, hidden away off the main street, is one of the most unusual in Derbyshire. An octagonal church, with a lantern roof on piers, was added to the original low, 15th century Perpendicular tower in 1759. It seems a strange mixture of styles, but it still manages to create a charming impression, with the congregation worshipping "in the round."

Just to the east of the church is **Stoney Middleton Hall**, the 17th century Jacobean former home of Lord Denman, Lord Chief Justice in 1832. Denman was a great Victorian reformer who advocated the abolition of slavery and who was the first national chairman of the Womens' Institute. He also famously defended Queen Caroline at her trial. Back on the Main Road, the octagonal **Toll House** of 1840 currently serves as the village "chippy."

Two wells are still dressed every summer.

Hannah's Leap

The village of Stoney Middleton is home to a legend of thwarted love and a spectacularly unsuccessful suicide bid. Local girl Hannah Badderley was jilted by her lover in 1762, and decided to end it all by leaping from a crag now known as Lover's Leap in Middleton Dale. Much to her despair, her voluminous skirt opened out like a parachute, got caught in some brambles where she hung suspended for a while, before she fell gently into a saw-pit, virtually unhurt.

Accommodation

Lists of various types of accommodation can be obtained from the Tourist Information Centre. There is a full range of serviced accommodation, including hotels, guest houses, bed and breakfasts, farm houses, a youth hostel in Hawkhill Road, Eyam (☎ 0845 371 9738) and camping and caravan sites.

Tourist Information Centre

Bakewell Visitor Centre
The Old Market Hall, Bridge Street, Bakewell, Derbyshire DE45 1DS
☎ 01629 816558; www.peakdistrict.gov.uk; open daily.

Doctors

Eyam Surgery
Church Street, Eyam, Hope Valley S32 5QH ☎ 01433 630836

Toilets and car park

There are public toilets and a pay-and-display car park in Hawkhill Road, Eyam. There is also a free car park above and behind the pay-and-display one. Donations towards the upkeep are welcome.

Attractions

Eyam Hall
Eyam, Hope Valley, Derbyshire S32 5QW ☎ 01433 631976; www.eyamhall.co.uk

Eyam Museum
Hawkhill Road, Eyam, Hope Valley, Derbyshire S32 5QP
☎ 01433 631371; www.eyam.org.uk

Published by **Ashbourne Editions**
Moor Farm Road West, Ashbourne, Derbyshire DE6 1HD
Tel: (01335) 347349 Fax: (01335) 347303

1st edition: ISBN: 978-1-873-775-36-3

© Roly Smith 2011

Printed
Gomer Press, Llandysul, Wales

Design
Mark Titterton – www.ceibagraphics.co.uk

Photography
© Mark Titterton
p.6 Courtesy of Eyam Museum Collection

Front Cover: Eyam Hall and stocks **Back cover top (l-r)**: Baslow, Catherine Mompesson's tomb – Eyam, The Eyre Arms – Hassop **Back cover main**: Eyam Moor **Page 1**: Padley Gorge